AF255659

THE BRANTFORD CALL

THE BRANTFORD CALL

–FOR DEEP CLEANSING WITHIN THE CHURCHES–

T. Hoogsteen

AFTERWORD BY

Yarman Halawa

RESOURCE *Publications* · Eugene, Oregon

THE BRANTFORD CALL
For Deep Cleansing within the Churches

Resource Publications
An Imprint of Wipf and Stock Publishers
199 W. 8th Ave., Suite 3
Eugene, OR 97401

www.wipfandstock.com

PAPERBACK ISBN: 978-1-7252-5920-1
HARDCOVER ISBN: 978-1-7252-5921-8
EBOOK ISBN: 978-1-7252-5922-5

Peter C. and Melody A.
For healing

Contents

Preface

In lax eras the Church eases into conformity with this world.
The faith of many then falters.

To take away descent into decadence,
Jesus,
the Head of the Church,
always reforms a remnant.

Since her origin Jesus separated and distinguished the Church from the
world.

Isaiah 51:1
Jeremiah 6:16a
Matthew 16:18

She is holy,
a people set apart,
and God the Father transforms her members into the likeness of his Son.

Deuteronomy 7:6–11, 12:29–31
Romans 8:10; 1 Corinthians 3:16–17; Colossians 1:13–14; Titus 2:11–14

Hence in seasons of falling faithfulness the Lord Jesus reforms her,
sanctifying;
he cleanses her of all hypocrisy.
Jesus, the Lord and Savior, decreed that all hasten to glorify him and the

Father in the Spirit.

\/

As you now meditate on the successive portions and savor
the individual parts,
One: may you hear Jesus's call to enter deep into holiness,
and Two: may the Spirit inspire you to long-lasting commitment
in sanctification.

\/

For the sake of clarity,
throughout *The Brantford Call** Scriptures constitute the infallible Word.

Deuteronomy 4:1–8, 32:1–3
John 20:30–31, 21:25
Romans 15:4; 2 Corinthians 4:1–3; 2 Timothy 3:16–17
2 Peter 1:16–24
1 John 1:1–4; Revelation 22:18–19

\/

Herewith I thank Rev. Mr. W. DenHollander and Rev. Dr. W. Koopmans,
brothers in the Faith and students of the Word,
for critical evaluations of this manuscript;
both improved the quality of *The Brantford Call.*

------

*Statements of faith regularly identify with places of origin:

The Belgic Confession. The Heidelberg Catechism. The Canons of Dort. The Westminster Standards. The London Baptist Confession of Faith. The Auburn Affirmation. The Wittenberg Witness. Chicago Statement on Biblical Inerrancy. The Belhar Confession. The Nashville Statement. New City Catechism.

THE RECREATED HEARING

1

The Church is holy to the Lord,
a people separated to glorify his holiness.
Jesus summons even hypocrites into the work of sanctification.

Deuteronomy 7:6–11
John 15:19, 17:14
1 Corinthians 3:16–17
1 Peter 2:9–10
Revelation 21:2

\/

From out of the beauty of holiness the Lord Jesus's call rings out:

You shall be holy;
for I the LORD your God am holy.

Leviticus 11:44–45, 19:2, 20:26, 22:31–33
Joshua 24:19
Isaiah 6:3

Again:

You shall be holy, for I am holy.

Matthew 5:8
1 Peter 1:16

To reinforce holiness the Lord Jesus's summoning permeates the Church,

regenerating hearts, souls, minds, and strengths,
all eventually to stand before him,
the glorious Judge.

Hearing, believers hear.

Everywhere
—in congregations, marriages/families, and schools—
whole communities listen and comply.
Throughout employment, social media, technology, citizenship, transportation, business, and recreation the holiness command requires immediate answer.

\/

The urgent imperative compels all in Christ at the crossroads onto the narrow way.

Deuteronomy 30:19–20
Joshua 24:14–15
Matthew 7:13–14; Luke 13:24
Hebrews 13:14

THE RECREATED SEEING

2

Barriers to holiness rise up from out of human hearts,
strong as prison bars.

Matthew 15:19; Mark 7:21–22
Romans 1:28–32; Galatians 5:19–23; 1 Timothy 1:8–11; Titus 1:10–11

Covetousness excites sinning to undo the coming of the Kingdom,
locking sinners behind bars of self-righteousness.

Psalms 73:4–9, 74:22–23, 83:1 8
Ecclesiastes 3:16–22
Isaiah 59:1–8
Malachi 3:5
Luke 13:10–17
2 Corinthians 12:20; Galatians 3:23–29, 5:19–21

evil thoughts	heartlessness	murder
ruthlessness	adultery	immorality
fornication	impurity	theft
idolatry	perjury	sorcery
slander	enmity	covetousness
jealousy	wickedness	anger
deceit	selfishness	licentiousness
dissension	envy	party spirit
pride	drunkenness	foolishness
carousing	evil	profanity

malice
homicide
malignity
sodomy
insolence
disobedience (to parent
misery
greed
alienation
angst
nazism/fascism
determinism
estrangement
decadence
despair
fanaticism
hatred
gluttony
gambling
genocide
religiosity
divorce
authoritarianism
thought crime
Buddhism
ignorance

patricide
strife
fratricide
hatred of God
haughtiness
faithlessness
lying
anguish
restlessness
racism
anti-intellectualism
meaninglessness
arms
nationalism
capitalism
chaos
papalism
socialism
paganism
lewdness
polygamy
pollution
communism
Islam
demonization
Gnosticism
discontent

femicide
matricide
gossiping
kidnapping
boastfulness
unfaithfulness
loneliness
dissatisfaction
opioid abuse
postmodernism
individualism
promiscuity
suffering
absolutism
epidemics
humanism
pornography
feminism
prejudice
pride
bitterness
political corruption
substance abuse
Hinduism
persecution
anxiety

Humanly speaking,
there is no way out from
behind these bars.

And believers?

Seeing, believers see.

Luke 6:43–45
John 8:34
Romans 6:15–19
2 Peter 2:17–22
Jude 17–23

THE SMART OF COVETOUSNESS

3

Adam stopped Eden's advance into the glories of the first eschaton;
he left Genesis 1:28 incomplete.
As head, the man chronically desecrated his righteousness,
the woman with him.

Genesis 3:1–7
Romans 5:12–14; 1 Corinthians 15:21–22; 1 Timothy 2:13–14

Created in holiness to will and to do righteousness,
the two ruined the original goodness for all human beings.

Genesis 1:31, 3:8–13

As one, the two called forth the Adamic sin,
covetousness,
the power of the flesh,
henceforth the Serpent's main assault weapon against the Christ.

Psalms 73:26, 119:120
Isaiah 40:6
Romans 7:4–6, 7:7–12, 8:3–8, 8:12–13; Galatians 5:16–17, 5:19–21, 6:7–10; Ephesians 2:11–12
1 Peter 2:11–12

Falling for the Devil's bargain,
covetous Adam and Eve called into existence all horrors
of self-justification,
the meaning and purpose of life locked in idolatries.

Every generation since has entered existence broken:
sealed behind prison bars,
committed to the Adamic sin,
intend on self-righteous strengths to excuse sinning.

Psalms 14:1–4, 53:1–5, 89:46–48
Ecclesiastes 9:13–16
Isaiah 1:4, 8:14–15, 30:8–14, 31:1–5, 47:8–9, 59:9–15
Jeremiah 17:9–10
Ezekiel 20:32
Amos 4:1–3, 6:1–3
Luke 12:54–56, 16:14–15
Romans 8:7–8; Ephesians 5:3–14; 2 Timothy 3:1–9
James 4:1–10

In the darkness of covetousness and its numerous denominations,
the glory of creation collapsed into the damnation of the Satan's snare.

Genesis 6:5, 11; Job 4:17
John 2:23–25
Romans 1:18–32, 3:9–20; 1 Timothy 3:7; 2 Timothy 3:1–9; Titus 1:10–14
2 Peter 2:4–10

JUSTIFICATION BY FAITH

THE RECREATED RIGHTEOUSNESS

4

With majestic holiness the Trinity pierces the hardiest blockades,
cleansing and reforming.

With majesty the Son reveals his holy omnipotence.

Exodus 3:5, 24:15–18, 40:34–35; Leviticus 9:23–24, 10:3; Deuteronomy 5:22–27,
6:20–25
Joshua 24:19
1 Samuel 2:2
1 Kings 8:10–13, 19:9–18
Psalm 85:4–7
Isaiah 5:24–25, 6:1–5, 43:3a, 55:5
Matthew 17:1–6; Mark 9:2–8
John 6:69
Acts 9:3–9
Galatians 3:23–29
Hebrews 4:12–13
2 Peter 1:17–19
Revelation 15:2–8, 19:13

Believers respond forthwith to the Lord Jesus's consecratory command.

Glory in his holy name;
let the hearts of those who seek the LORD rejoice!

1 Chronicles 16:10, 16:28–34

With majesty the Father through the Son reveals his holy omnipotence.

John 17:11
1 Timothy 6:15–16
James 1:16–18
Revelation 4:3, 4:8, 21:22–23

With majesty the Spirit through the Father and the Son reveals his holy
omnipotence.

Isaiah 63:10
Acts 10:44–45, 11:23–24, 15:8–9
1 Peter 1:10–12
Revelation 3:1

As one, the Son, the Father, and the Spirit,
future-minded,
draw the elect into his transcendent holiness.

Psalm 125:3c
2 Peter 1:3–11

5

The one God reveals his holiness in righteousness.

In holiness the Son wills and does righteousness.

Genesis 1:1–31; Exodus 20:1–17
Psalms 22:3–5, 33:4–5, 36:5–6, 50:6, 85:10, 89:14, 103:6–14, 118:19, 119:137
Isaiah 11:5, 45:21, 45:23, 59:17
Jeremiah 23:6, 33:15
John 6:37–40, 7:16–18, 8:29
Romans 5:17; Galatians 3:10–14; Colossians 2:6
Hebrews 1:1–4, 4:11–13
James 4:13–17
1 John 2:1–2

In holiness the Father wills and does righteousness.

John 17:25
Acts 17:29–31
Romans 1:17, 3:21–22; 1 Corinthians 1:30; Colossians 1:24–29; 1 Timothy 6:14–16
1 Peter 1:3–5, 1:17
1 John 3:1–3
Revelation 4:1–11

In holiness the Spirit wills and does righteousness.

Acts 5:1–11
Romans 8:2, 8:11, 8:14, 15:19–21; 1 Corinthians 2:10
1 Peter 1:10–12

\/

In trinitarian unity the Three reveal the consecratory power now at work
in the Church,

based on the promises he gave the *very good* Adam,
which if broken revealed death.

Genesis 2:17

These promises instituted the foundation for the Gospel in all generations:

the first, life,

Genesis 1:26–27

the second, food,

Genesis 1:29

and the third, space.

Genesis 2:8

6

From out of the glory of the divine holiness the Lord Jesus
created justification,
its imputation by fiat* only.
This righteous judgment recreated a people to will and to do the works of
rectitude.
Within the Church he compels all to believe justification by faith.
This is the sole exit out of the darkness.

Genesis 15:6
Habakkuk 2:4b
Romans 1:16–17, 3:21–26, 3:27–31, 5:1–5

The Judge of all the earth revealed on Golgotha the unmerited favor of the
great judgment:

You are righteous, for all eternity!

Thus he handed down the sentence of justification with the actuality of
grace.
This is the almighty fiat from the Cross,
the First and Great Judgment.

Psalms 32:1–2, 33:4–5
John 3:18–21
Romans 4:7–8, 4:23–25, 5:15–17, 5:18–21, 6:15–19, 8:1–8; 2 Corinthians 4:6; Gala-
tians 3:6–9; Ephesians 2:1–2
Hebrews 13:12

Here in the Church—and here alone—is the access into holiness.

Jesus's imputation of grace the sovereign Father accepts and the sovereign
Spirit implements.

Now Christians believe the Gospel's covenant promises:

of life,

Exodus 3:7–12, 12:1–20
Isaiah 40:1–2, 52:3
John 1:29, 3:36, 14:8–11, 17:24
Romans 10:10

of food,

Exodus 3:17, 16:13, 16:15
Psalm 111:5
Matthew 14:13–21, 15:32–39; Mark 6:35–44, 8:1–10; John 6:1–14
1 Corinthians 11:23–26

and of space.

Genesis 45:6–11
Exodus 3:7–10; Numbers 33:50–56; Deuteronomy 1:8, 6:10–15
Psalm 111:6
Romans 4:13

With the holiness of grace the Christ broke into the confines of idolatry,
imputing to believers that which his own never earned.

Exodus 15:13
Psalm 70:4
John 12:44–50
Romans 3:21–26, 11:5; Galatians 3:23–29
Hebrews 4:14–16

------

*A command or act of the will without apparent effort.
A dictate or sentence at the bar of justice.
"Let it be done!"

SANCTIFICATION IN FAITH

THE RECREATED HOLINESS

7

The Christ prepared himself to reveal the teaching of justification.
Thereto he structured the history of the world out of prophetic Genesis
3:14–19,
the first dispensation of which inscripturated as the Old Testament.

Justification re-initiates human holiness.

In faith all believers:

put on the Christ,

Galatians 3:27

have the Christ in them,

John 17:23
Romans 8:10; 2 Corinthians 3:3; Galatians 2:20; Ephesians 3:17; Colossians 1:27,
3:3–4

and live in Christ.

Romans 8:1–2, 14:8; 1 Corinthians 4:10, 6:17; 2 Corinthians 12:2; Galatians 4:19

All with Christ Jesus in the heart,
all with the youthful intensity of Isaiah 40:27–31,
and all with childlike trust ever more believe the narrative of Jesus's Person and ministry.

Psalms 73:26, 85:10–13
Isaiah 55:6–9
Luke 1:1–4
2 Corinthians 4:6

Trusting with indelible intensity the narrative of the Christ's Person and
ministry,
—Genesis-Revelation—
all find that daily he pours more holiness into new wineskins.

Matthew 9:16–17; Luke 5:36–39

Thus from within begins and matures the new life,
the new creation inside each believer.

John 6:40, 15:1–11, 17:17
Romans 6:4, 8, 10, 7:22, 8:16; 2 Corinthians 4:16; Ephesians 3:16, 4:22–24; Colossians 3:10

Know this then:

THE LESS KNOWN AND BELIEVED OF JESUS IN HIS MINISTRY,
THE EASIER ASSIMILATION INTO THE WORLD
AND
THE MORE BELIEVED AND KNOWN OF JESUS IN HIS MINISTRY,
THE STRONGER SANCTIFICATION IN HOLINESS.

Psalm 145:13–20
Matthew 7:24–27
1 Corinthians 1:18–25
2 Peter 3:18
Revelation 3:15–19

8

To achieve the Incarnation, he selected Abraham's descendants.

Deuteronomy 7:6–8
1 Chronicles 16:14–18
Matthew 1:1
Romans 4:17; Galatians 3:6–9, 3:29
James 2:21

En route, through the first dispensation he foretold in the Old Church his
coming in the flesh.

Genesis 3:14–15, 22:1–19
Deuteronomy 18:15–22
2 Samuel 7:12–13
Psalm 132:11–12
Isaiah 7:14/Matthew 1:23
Isaiah 9:2–7, 11:1–3, 11:10, 28:16–17, 42:1–4/Matthew 12:18–21, 52:13—53:12,
61:1–4/Luke 4:18–19
Jeremiah 23:6, 31:31–34
Ezekiel 1:26–28, 36:22–32
Hosea 11:1
Micah 5:2
Zechariah 2:6–10, 6:9–14, 9:9/Luke 19:38
Malachi 3:2b–4

In the majesty of holiness* the LORD God
—omnipotent and omniscient—
with the Father and in the Spirit prepared Mary,
and his Israelite body.

Matthew 1:18–23; Luke 1:26–35, 1:41–45
John 1:14
Galatians 4:4–5
Hebrews 10:5–7

From within the tumult of nations and empires he breaks open the way,
majestically,
for the salvation of the Church and the coming of the Kingdom.

Psalms 65:5–8, 89:9, 93:3–4, 98:7–9
Isaiah 9:1–2/Matthew 4:15–17, 34:1–4, 45:9–13, 51:15
Daniel 7:1–7
Luke 1:14–17, 1:67–79, 2:29–35, 21:25–28
John 8:23
Acts 4:23–31/Psalm 2:1–11
Revelation 18:1–24

------

*Of the transferable attributes: holiness, righteousness, love, mercy, good-
ness, and grace, even veracity, spirituality, truthfulness, wisdom, knowledge, and sovereignty.

Of the nontransferable attributes: transcendence, aseity, immutability, in-
finity, eternity, omnipotence, omniscience, and trinitarian unity.

9

In the linear ascent of Old Testament history,
the Preincarnate, by grace, initiated covenantal righteousness.

Beginning with Abraham (and Sarah),

Genesis 17:1,

he recreated in his own the will and the ability to believe the great teach-
ings of the Scriptures,
each always with respect to holiness.

Genesis 15:6/Romans 4:5b
Joshua 24:16–22
Psalm 32:1–2
Isaiah 51:1–2
Habakkuk 2:4b/Romans 1:17
I Corinthians 3:16–17; Galatians 3:6; 1 Thessalonians 2:1–4
1 Peter 2:4–5

The Christ, with the Father and in the Spirit, created a movable horizon.
On this horizon he appointed days of judgment,
dread unimaginable,
each a day of the Lord.

Isaiah 2:2–5, 2:20–22, 13:9–16, 30:27–28, 42:5–9, 51:4–6, 60:8–14, 65:17–25,
66:22–23
Joel 1:15, 2:1–2, 2:11, 2:31, 3:14
Amos 5:18–20, 8:1–3, 8:9–10
Micah 4:1–5
Zephaniah 1:7–9, 1:14–16
Malachi 3:1–4, 4:1–3
Matthew 24:1–51; Mark 13:1–37; Luke 12:49–53, 17:22–37, 21:5–36

Acts 2:19–21
1 Corinthians 1:8; 1 Thessalonians 5:2
1 Peter 4:7–11; 2 Peter 3:8–19
Revelation 19:11–16

On those days he cleansed the covenant community of all reprobates,
as well as gave the lie to false prophets.

1 Kings 18:20–29, 22:1–28; 2 Kings 3:13
Jeremiah 5:10–13, 5:30–31, 14:13–16, 28:1–4
Ezekiel 13:1–7
Micah 2:6–11, 3:5–8
Matthew 24:11, 24:24; Mark 13:22
Acts 20:29–30
1 Corinthians 4:5; 2 Timothy 3:1–11
2 Peter 2:1–3, 3:1–7
1 John 2:26–27; 2 John 7
Jude 4

10

On the day of the Lord,
at the natal hour, the incarnate Christ came forth.

Matthew 1:18-21; Luke 2:1–7, 2:8–15; John 6:29
Galatians 4:4; Philippians 2:5–7
Revelation 12:1–6

He is sinless from conception on.

Hebrews 4:15, 7:26, 9:14
1 Peter 2:22
1 John 3:5

Through the power of the Holy Spirit, God the Son assumed flesh,
a humanly incomprehensible work.

Matthew 1:18–25; Luke 1:26–35; John 1:14
Philippians 2:5–11
Hebrews 2:9, 2:14–18
Revelation 12:1–6

For the Incarnation Day the Spirit qualified him and the Father sent him.

John 1:1–5, 3:31–36, 5:37–38, 17:25
Acts 13:33

The Son,
God and man,
willed this awe-inspiring event:
dwelling among his own,
to the horror of the nations.

Psalm 2:1–2

Sanctification In Faith

Matthew 2:1–23
Acts 4:23–31
Revelation 12:1–6, 12:12

The immensity of the Incarnation astonishes still rising covenant generations:
God on earth among his people in the Church.

Matthew 1:22–23
2 Corinthians 8:9; Philippians 2:6–7

In respective Gospels, Matthew, Mark, Luke, and John,
centered on Jesus in his redemptive work for the recreation of holiness in
his people.

11

With the Baptizer, Jesus began his ministry.

Malachi 3:1–4, 4:5–6
Matthew 3:1–17, 11:11–15, 17:9–13; Mark 1:1–11; Luke 3:1–22
John 1:6–8, 1:15, 3:22–30, 5:33–36

God the Son
—in the Jordan and under the waters of baptism—
assumed the burden of the Oral Law,*
Israel's dominating sin,
wherewith they of the covenant coveted self-righteousness.

Matthew 15:1–9, 23:1–36; Mark 7:1–8; Luke 11:37–44
Galatians 3:13; Philippians 3:2b–3

\/

The dark god possessed the Church,
full of promising ways to self-justification.

Genesis 3:1–7
Job 1:6–12
Isaiah 14:12–21
Ezekiel 28:11–19
Zechariah 3:1–5
John 8:38, 8:44, 13:27
Acts 16:16–18
2 Corinthians 11:12–15; Ephesians 6:10–17
1 Peter 5:6–11
1 John 3:4–10
Revelation 12:13–17

Since the dawn the Satan promised to gratify the flesh.

Flesh through covetousness wanted satisfaction by sinning.

Genesis 3:1–7
Romans 8:5–8; Galatians 5:11–17; Philippians 3:3

\/

Jesus in his first public work revealed the Trinity:
The Father and the Spirit vowed to protect the Son in his humanity.

Matthew 3:13–17; Mark 1:9–11; Luke 3:21–22, 4:18–19; John 1:18, 1:29–34,
12:27–33
James 4:7b

Thus Christ Jesus,
with his sovereign divinity supporting his humanity and with the Father's
omnipotence,
entered upon the way to Golgotha for the grace of imputed justification.

Matthew 16:13–20, 17:1–8; Mark 8:27–33; Luke 9:18–22, 9:28–36; John 6:68–69,
7:41, 12:29–34
2 Peter 1:16–24

The Incarnate made his humanity repeatedly visible:

Anger

Mark 3:5

Disgust

Mark 8:12

Distress

John 12:27

Affection

Mark 9:36

Sorrow

John 11:35

Sympathy

Hebrews 4:15

------

*The Oral Law consisted of the legal tradition the Jews invented after the
Exile.
This other law served Pharisees/Sadducees to gain an impossible self-
righteousness.

12

Jesus foretold the fact of the Crucifixion.

Isaiah 52:13—53:12
Matthew 16:21–23, 26:2; Mark 9:30–32; Luke 18:31–34; John 12:33

Consequently,
in a ministry of inconceivable suffering,
he walked—according to Mark—from Galilee into Jerusalem,
planning the trials and the verdicts.

Matthew 26:57–68; Mark 14:53–65; Luke 22:66–71; John 18:12–14, 18:19–24,
18:28—19:16
Matthew 27:11–26; Mark 15:1–20; Luke 23:1–5, 23:6–12, 23:13–24

\/

To his suffering in Gethsemane he added Judas Iscariot's betrayal.

Psalm 41:9/John 13:18, Psalm 55:12–15
Matthew 26:14–16/Zechariah 11:12; Matthew 26:47–56, 27:3–10
John 6:70–71, 13:21–30, 17:12b, 18:1–4
Acts 1:18–20

Peter also increased Jesus's suffering by denying him.

Matthew 26:30–35, 26:69–75; Mark 14:26–31, 14:66–72, Luke 22:31–34, 22:56–62

\/

This was the Son of man's hour.

Psalm 8:4

Ezekiel 2:1
Matthew 26:64; Mark 14:21, 62; Luke 21:27, 21:25–28, 22:69

At the appointed hour, the Judge's judges accused him of blasphemy.

Matthew 26:57–68; Mark 14:53–65; Luke 22:66–71

Moreover, the Roman government condemned him on a contrived charge of treason.

Matthew 27:11–14; Mark 15:6–15; Luke 23:1–25; John 18:33–38, 19:1–16
Matthew 27:37; Mark 15:26; Luke 23:38; John 19:19

The courts committed him—the Christ—to the Roman death for sedition.
Then he walked to Golgotha to become sin.

Matthew 27:32–34; Mark 15:16–32; Luke 23:32–38
2 Corinthians 5:21; Colossians 2:13–14; 1 Timothy 1:15
1 Peter 1:18–20

For this he had come:
To atone for the guilt of sinning,
his life a ransom for many.

Matthew 20:28; Mark 10:45
1 Corinthians 6:20, 7:23; 1 Timothy 2:6

Throughout, he kept the wholeness of his bones and of his consciousness,
refusing a sedative.

Deuteronomy 21:22–23
Psalms 34:20, 69:21
Mark 15:23; Luke 23:36

13

All sinning originated in covetousness.
In every present the Lord calls all to account for covetousness.

Genesis 3:1–7, 4:8–12
Romans 8:7–8

\/

Sinning misses the mark of righteousness and holiness.

Exodus 10:16, 32:33; Deuteronomy 1:41
Matthew 7:6; Luke 15:18
2 Peter 2:10a–22

Sinning occurs through ignorance.

Exodus 23:33; Numbers 14:41; Deuteronomy 4:28
Leviticus 4:1–3, 4:13–14, 4:22–24, 4:27–28
Psalm 58:3
Acts 17:30

Sinning is revolution, rebellion, and transgression.

Leviticus 16:21; Numbers 16:1–50
1 Kings 12:19
Isaiah 66:3–5
Jeremiah 11:9–13
Ezekiel 3:4–11
Daniel 8:1–14
Amos 1:1—2:3
Acts 5:39, 7:51–53
2 Peter 2:4

Sinning is to be wrong or perverted, even do wrong or act perversely.

Genesis 19:15
Isaiah 24:1–3, 32:3
Colossians 3:25; 2 Timothy 3:1–9

Sinning displays inner badness, worthlessness.

Genesis 38:10, 48:17
Deuteronomy 15:9
Matthew 12:45, 16:4; Luke 13:6–9

Sinning is to be wicked.

Psalm 1:4
Isaiah 57:20
Zechariah 5:5–11
1 Peter 3:17

Sinning lacks integrity and rectitude.

Isaiah 65:11–12
Matthew 10:32–33, 12:30; Mark 7:18–23; Luke 11:23
James 2:10

Sinning breaks out against authority.

Number 12:1–8
Proverbs 4:24
Jeremiah 17:9
Matthew 15:19; Luke 6:45
Hebrews 3:12

Sinning follows evil courses.

Genesis 3:1–7
Isaiah 48:8
Jeremiah 14:10, 18:12
1 John 3:4

Sinning incurs guilt and is the door to hell.

Deuteronomy 24:16
2 Chronicles 25:4
Ezekiel 18:10–13

Matthew 5:22
Romans 6:23, 7:13

Sinning is lawlessness.

1 John 3:4–10

Sinning is treasonous.

2 Samuel 15:7–12, 20:1–2
1 Kings 1:9–10, 2:13–18, 11:13

\/

None legitimately plead ignorance.

Deuteronomy 21:22–23
Psalm 19:1–6
2 Samuel 16:7
1 Kings 2:39–46
Isaiah 55:1–5, 63:15–19, 64:8
Romans 1:18–23

14

At the appointed hour on Crucifixion Day,
cross-nailed and supported by his divinity,
Jesus in his humanity absorbed at one and the same time tripled condemnation:

the Father's wrath against the Church's sinning,

Romans 1:18, 5:9; Ephesians 2:3; 1 Thessalonians 5:9
Revelation 16:1

the Spirit's wrath against the Church's sinning,

Isaiah 63:10–14
Luke 12:10; Acts 5:1–11
Ephesians 4:30; 1 Thessalonians 5:19

and the Son's wrath against the Church's sinning.

Exodus 22:21–24
Isaiah 51:17, 63:5
Jeremiah 6:11, 10:10; Lamentations 4:11
Ezekiel 13:15
Hosea 13:9
Nahum 1:6
Habakkuk 3:2
Matthew 12:31–32; Luke 12:10
Galatians 3:10, 3:13

Rejected by the Church,
forsaken by the Father,
and condemned on the authority of Roman Empire,
Jesus in agonies beyond pain created the atonement to overcome sinners'
self-righteousness.

Thus he suffered the condemnation his people had earned for profaning
the covenant promises.

Deuteronomy 21:22–23
Psalm 22:1–2
Matthew 27:26, 27:45–50; Mark 15:15, 15:33–39; Luke 23:24–25, 23:44–49; John
19:1–16
Acts 2:22–23
Romans 8:3; 1 Thessalonians 2:14–16
Hebrews 5:7, 13:11–13
1 Peter 4:1

For the cleansing of the Church, he shed his blood.

Leviticus 17:11
Matthew 26:28; Mark 14:24; John 6:53
Romans 5:9, 6:10; 1 Corinthians 11:25
Hebrews 9:13–14
1 Peter 1:1–2
1 John 1:6–7, 1:18–19
Revelation 1:5b, 7:14

This satisfied all divine justice for the redemption of Jesus's own.

\/

In the humility of and with the suffering on the Cross,
God the Son* and the Son of God** endured all hellish agonies in place of
the elect.

He is the Savior.

Isaiah 43:3, 43:11, 45:15, 60:16
Luke 2:11; John 1:9–13, 3:16–17, 4:42, 19:17–22
Acts 13:23
Romans 5:6–11; Philippians 3:20; Titus 2:11, 2:13, 3:3–7
Hebrews 9:23–28
1 John 4:1–4

He is the Deliverer.

Psalms 14:7, 18:2
Isaiah 59:20
Romans 11:26–27; Ephesians 1:3–14

He is the Redeemer.

Job 19:25
Psalm 19:14
Isaiah 41:14, 44:6–8, 47:4, 60:16

He is the Reconciler.

Romans 5:10; 2 Corinthians 5:16–21; Ephesians 2:16; Colossians 1:20

He is the Christ, the Messiah.

Matthew 16:16, 22:42; Luke 9:20; John 1:41, 4:25
Acts 2:36
1 Corinthians 1:24; 2 Corinthians 5:19; Ephesians 5:2

He issued the First Judgment and recreated the dividing-line.

Psalms 75:6–8, 94:1–3
Isaiah 61:8–9
Malachi 4:1-3
Matthew 25:1–46
John 3:18–21, 12:31–32
Colossians 1:21–23
Revelation 14:13

----

*God the Son signifies his divinity.

Matthew 11:27, 27:54; John 1:14, 3:16–17, 19:7
Romans 1:3, 8:3; 1 Corinthians 1:9; Colossians 1:13

**Son of God signifies his saviorhood.

John 1:34, 49
Acts 9:20
Romans 1:4

15

Jesus's followers entombed his body,
the evidence of his death.

Matthew 27:50; Mark 15:37; Luke 23:46; John 19:30
Matthew 27:55–61; Mark 15:42–47; Luke 23:50–56; John 19:31–42

It is finished.

Deuteronomy 21:22–23
Joshua 8:29, 10:26–27
Psalms 16:10, 116:3
Isaiah 53:9
Hosea 13:14
Acts 2:29–36, 13:29
I Corinthians 15:3–4, 15:42–50, 15:51–57

\/

In his death and burial Jesus sanctified respective graves,
remembering the places of all bodies.

\/

While his body rested in the sepulcher,
a stone sealed off the enclosed space.

Matthew 27:62–66; Mark 15:42–47; Luke 23:50–56; John 19:38–42

Jesus proclaimed to all in Sheol/Hades condemnation long remembered.
He held the rebellious spirits accountable,
offering no reprieve.

Isaiah 5:13–17
1 Peter 3:19, 4:6

In the Eschaton they face, with all unbelievers living, the inescapable eternities of condemnation.

Isaiah 26:19
Ezekiel 37:12
Daniel 12:2
Matthew 25:46; John 5:28–29
Revelation 20:11–14

16

On Resurrection Day,
after three days and nights of death,
the Trinity revealed the Resurrection:

Jesus created the Resurrection.*

Psalm 116:3
Jonah 1:17
Matthew 16:21, 26:61, 28:11–10; Mark 16:1–8; Luke 24:1–12; John 2:18–22,
10:17–18, 11:25, 20:1–10

The Father created the Resurrection.

John 5:21, 5:25–30, 6:40
Acts 2:24/Psalm 16:9–10; Acts 2:32, 3:15, 5:30, 10:40, 13:30–35
Romans 8:9–11, 10:9; Ephesians 1:20; Colossians 2:12
1 Peter 1:3–5

The Spirit created the Resurrection.

Romans 1:4, 8:11

The Three as One executed absolute sovereignty over life and death.
Thus, the Divinity created the Resurrection,
glorifying the Son's humanity.

1 Corinthians 15:3–11

But someone will ask, "How are the dead raised?"

1 Corinthians 15:35–50

The Resurrection is:
The recreation of Jesus's human nature,
thereby breaking the bondage of sin and death,
an inaccessibly complex trinitarian work,
revealed only to the eschatologically bound Church.
He in life and in death is her *Yes* and *Amen*.

1 Corinthians 15:42–50
2 Corinthians 1:19–20

\/

The Resurrection reveals Jesus's conquest over sin and death,
generating in his own the hope of the resurrection.

Psalm 118:22–23/Mark 12:10–11
Isaiah 25:8, 26:19
Daniel 12:2
Hosea 13:14
John 5:21, 5:25, 5:29
1 Corinthians 15:26–28, 15:54–55; 2 Corinthians 4:16—5:15; 2 Timothy 1:8–10
1 Peter 1:3–5
Revelation 1:17–20, 20:4–6, 20:13

------

*Jesus's authority over death:

1 Kings 17:17–24; 2 Kings 4:32–37, 13:20–21
Matthew 9:18–26, 27:51–53; Mark 5:35–43; Luke 7:11–17; John 11:38–44
Acts 9:40, 20:7–12
Hebrews 2:14–15

17

Over forty days,
Jesus ate and drank with the Twelve,*
revealing to them the factuality of the Resurrection,
which the Apostles taught the New Church.

John 7:32–36, 14:1–7, 14:18–20, 14:27–31, 16:5–11, 17:1–5, 20:11–28
Acts 1:1–5, 1:6–11, 10:41
1 Corinthians 15:1–11, 15:20–23, 15:50

Moreover, he laid the foundation of the New Church,
on which he taught the essence of justification by faith and the glories of
holiness.

1 Corinthians 3:10–11; Ephesians 2:20; 2 Timothy 2:19
Revelation 21:14

\/

On Ascension Day Jesus ascended to his Father's right hand,
his throne since the Creation.

Psalms 24:7–10, 47:5–7
Luke 24:50–53
Acts 1:6–11
Ephesians 1:20
Hebrews 1:1–4
Revelation 5:6–10/Daniel 7:9–14

The reputable Twelve witnessed the factuality of his inexplicable ascension.
Thus Jesus in his Person's divinity/humanity revealed the reunion of
heaven and earth.

Within the new dispensation Jesus initiated eschatological haste:

Come, Lord Jesus!

Acts 2:19–21
1 Corinthians 7:31b, 16:21
Revelation 20:1–3, 22:20

His mercy is new every morning.

Lamentations 3:22–23
Isaiah 54:9–10
Zechariah 1:12–17
Matthew 24:38–39; Luke 17:26–30

------

*Minus Judas Iscariot

Matthew27:3–10; Acts 1:15–20

and before Matthias's assignment.

Acts 1:26.

18

On Pentecost Day,
the Holy Spirit descended upon the original New Testament congregation,
a promise accomplished.

Matthew 3:11; Mark 1:8; Luke 3:16
Acts 1:15–16, 2:1–4

The Spirit brings to bear on the New Church
—to a people set apart and still prone to moral vice—
the glory of the divine holiness.

Deuteronomy 16:9–12
1 Chronicles 16:35–36
Psalms 46:4–7, 48:1–3
Isaiah 12:3–4, 45:14–17
Zechariah 4:1–10
John 15:18–25, 20:19–23
Acts 1:4–5, 2:33, 10:44–48, 19:6
Ephesians 1:15–23

He is the other Counsellor.

John 14:15–17, 14:25–26, 15:26–27, 16:7–11, 16:12–15

The glory of holiness believers reflect in the humility that justification by
faith inspires:
trusting in Jesus Christ and believing the Trinity.

Now to a whole and integral people undiminished in righteousness:

And in the last days it shall be,
God declares,

that I will pour out my Spirit on all flesh,
and your sons and your daughters shall prophesy,
and your young men shall see visions,
and your old men shall dream dreams;
even on my male servants and female servants I will pour out my Spirit,
and they shall prophesy.

Joel 2:28–29
John 7:37–39
Acts 2:17–18
1 John 4:13–21

In the Spirit the New Church moves on.

Isaiah 44:1–5, 63:3–9
Acts 2:5–13, 2:43–47, 5:32
Romans 8:9–11, 8:12–17; Galatians 5:5; Ephesians 1:13–14; Colossians 3:1–4

19

In the full revelation of his holiness,
Jesus, with the Father and in the Spirit, revealed himself.

He is the King of kings and the Lord of lords.

Deuteronomy 17:14–20
Psalms 24:7, 29:1–11, 47:7–9, 61:6–7, 72:1–19, 99:4–5, 105:1–3, 136:1–3, 138:4–6,
145:4–7, 145:13
Isaiah 6:1–5, 11:3–5, 40:12–17, 41:14–16, 43:15
Matthew 21:5
Philippians 2:9–11/Isaiah 45:23
Hebrews 13:8
Revelation 17:14, 19:16

He is the Creator.*

Job 38:4–7
Psalms 104:24, 135:6–7
Jeremiah 10:12–14
John 1:2–3
I Corinthians 8:6; Colossians 1:15–16
Hebrews 1:10–14, 2:10

He is the Judge.

Deuteronomy 1:17, 24:16, 25:1–3, 32:39–42
Judges 2:16
Psalms 7:6–8, 7:11, 72:2, 98:9
Micah 4:3
Malachi 3:2–3
John 2:28–29, 5:25–29
Acts 10:42
Romans 2:16; 2 Timothy 4:1
James 4:12, 5:9

1 Peter 4:5
Revelation 20:4–6

He is the Shepherd.

Psalms 23:1–6, 80:1
Isaiah 40:11
Jeremiah 3:15, 23:1–4
Ezekiel 34:1–31, 37:24–28
Micah 7:14
John 10:7–18
Hebrews 13:20–21
1 Peter 5:4

He is the Commander.

Deuteronomy 25:17–19
Joshua 5:13–15
2 Samuel 22:1–51
Isaiah 42:10–13
Revelation 19:11–16

He is the Mediator.

1 Timothy 2:5
Hebrews 12:24

He is the Intercessor.

Romans 8:34
Hebrews 4:14–16, 7:25, 9:24
1 John 2:1–2

He is the Husband.

Isaiah 54:4–13, 61:10–11
Jeremiah 2:1–3
Revelation 19:6–8, 21:1–4

\/

Jesus is the omniscient Prophet.
Following Moses's calling, he ineffably structured and taught all to come.

Deuteronomy 18:15–22, 34:10–12

Matthew 10:41, 11:9
Acts 3:22–26, 7:37

\/

Jesus is the Priest.
After Aaron's calling Jesus revealed himself the Sacrifice to gain the salvation of his own.

Exodus 28:1
Psalm 110:4
Hebrews 7:11–22, 7:23–25

His own put on holiness to honor the one Lord and Savior.

------

*God the Father also created.

Revelations 4:11
Hosea 2:14–23
Revelation 4:11, 21:1–4

THE RECREATED SPACE

20

In the space granted the Church, the Lord Jesus creates faith,
that inherent human capacity to believe him at his command.

Matthew 4:12–17; Mark 1:14–15; Luke 4:14–15
John 14:1–3
Acts 16:31
Romans 1:5, 16:26; 2 Thessalonians 1:8
1 John 3:23

Faith is the major constituent of the image of God in all people.
By faith believers hear and trust the Lord Jesus's imputed justification,
which he with the Father and through the Spirit inserts into the elect.

Romans 3:21–26, 4:11–12, 4:16–25

And you,
who were dead in trespasses and the uncircumcision of your flesh,
God made alive together with [the Christ],
having forgiven us all our trespasses,
having cancelled the bond which stood against us with its legal demands;
this he set aside, nailing it to the cross.

Acts 10:43
Galatians 2:19–21; Colossians 2:13–14

Faith begins in the Church.
Faith finds motivation at home.
Faith gains intellectual maturity in worship and through schooling.

Faith generates earnestness in living,
joy too.

Acts 10:34–43, 15:8–9
Romans 4:9, 6:1, 10:8–9, 10:17/Isaiah 52:7; 1 Corinthians 5:7; 1 Thessalonians
5:12–22
Hebrews 11:1, 12:12–17
James 1:21, 2:14–16, 4:8
2 Peter 1:9–11
1 John 1:9

Faith creates thinking, learning, speaking, working, and emoting,
giving the vigor of holiness meaning and purpose.

Believing Jesus's history motivates serving the Lord and Savior in consecration.
Believers then abandon all powers of covetousness and press onwards for
total sanctification.

Philippians 2:12–13, 3:12–16
Colossians 3:12–17
Jude 3

Believing fights hesitation and doubt.

Matthew 6:30, 8:26, 14:31, 21:21
Romans 14:23
James 1:5–7, 2:14–26
Jude 22

In the second dispensation the Lord Jesus,
with the Father and in the Spirit,
leads the believing Church into the Eschaton.

All others he leaves behind, gathering the evidence of reprobation.

2 Thessalonians 2:11–12
Revelation 17:17

21

Christ Jesus from earliest times revealed his Office: King, Prophet, and Priest. These three he distributed throughout the Church for her structure and organization.

He is the King.

Zechariah 9:9/Matthew 21:5; Luke 1:33
Revelation 17:13–14, 19:16

He is the Prophet.

Matthew 13:57; John 1:18, 15:15
Acts 3:22/Deuteronomy 18:15, 7:37

He is the Priest.

John 1:29
Psalm 110:4/Hebrews 7:17
Romans 8:34
Hebrews 9:11–14, 10:11–14
1 John 2:1
Revelation 5:6

\/

In the Church, Jesus rules each congregation by office bearers:

Elders he mandates with oversight of the preaching, discipline, and mis-sions.

John 4:35–38, 17:20–26
1 Corinthians 5:9–13; Galatians 1:6–9; 1 Thessalonians 5:12–13; 1 Timothy 1:8–11,
3:1–7, 5:17–22; Titus 1:5–9, 1:10–16

Hebrews 12:3–11/Proverbs 3:11–12, 13:17
1 Peter 2:11–12, 5:1–5

Ministers he mandates with prophesying,
in his name to proclaim all great doctrines and all holy living.

Isaiah 45:22–23, 48:3–5, 48:6–8, 49:5–7, 52:7, 55:10–11, 56:6–8, 60:1–3, 66:2
Jeremiah 1:10
Ezekiel 3:16–21, 18:1–32, 33:1–9
Matthew 7:15–20, 13:1–8, 28:16–20; Mark 4:1–9; Luke 8:4–8; John 8:47, 8:51
Acts 5:29, 20:26–29
Romans 10:14–21; 1 Corinthians 4:1, 15:12–19; 2 Corinthians 2:14–17; 1 Timothy
3:14–16, 5:17b
Hebrews 3:7–11, 4:11–13, 13:7
James 1:16–18

Deacons he mandates to alleviate hunger, poverty, homelessness, and
dispossession,
first among a congregation's own widows, orphans, and sojourners to
unify every Body.

Number 18:1–32
Psalms 68:5–6, 82:3–4, 146:5–9
Proverbs 30:7–9
Isaiah 10:1–4, 58:6–9
Jeremiah 7:5–7
Amos 4:1–3, 8:4–6
Zechariah 7:8–14
Malachi 3:5
Acts 4:32–37, 20:35
1 Timothy 5:3–8, 5:9–16
James 1:26–27

Deacons care for neighbors too,
calling governments to commit to social justice for the poor and margin-
alized.

Ecclesiastes 4:1–3
1 Timothy 3:8–13

By elders, ministers, and deacons,
—men Spirit-equipped for office bearing—
the Christ leads the Church out of moral depravities into the Eschaton,
in the process transforming his people into communities of wholeness.

Psalm 68:32–35
Exodus 19:22; Numbers 17:1—11
Acts 2:43–47, 4:32–37
Galatians 6:10

For strengthening the faith founded on and build up by the preaching
Jesus added sacraments:

22

The Church administers baptism once in the name of the Triune God;
Jesus commands the sprinkling by or immersion into water for all members of the Church,
thus to impress on each, as soon as feasible, the covenant sign and seal.

Genesis 17:9–14
Luke 1:59, 2:21
Acts 2:39
1 Corinthians 10:1–5
Titus 3:3–7
1 Peter 3:21–22

Parents thereto engage in self-examination preparatory to the sacrament.
Believing adults submit to this sacrament in a responsible manner.

This sacrament is circumcision reformed.

Deuteronomy 10:16, 30:6
Jeremiah 4:4
Romans 2:29, 4:1
Colossians 2:11–12

This sacrament declares the way ahead:

I am the way, and the truth, and the life.

Genesis 17:1
John 14:6
Acts 8:26–40, 16:25–34
Romans 6:1–3
Colossians 3:11

Every baptism in the congregation reminds and strengthens believers in justification by faith.

53

23

The Lord's Supper Jesus instituted to reform the Passover.

Exodus 12:1–13
2 Kings 23:21–23
2 Chronicles 30:1–27, 35:1–19
Ezra 6:19–22
Matthew 26:20–29; Mark 14:17–25; Luke 22:14–23
I Corinthians 10:14–22, 11:23–26

Upon justification by faith this sacrament fortifies believers to persevere in
sanctification,
perpetually focusing attention on the source of the Church's origin, life,
and vigor;
that is,
Christ Jesus's incarnation, death, resurrection, and his continuing rule,
to accentuate the new and eternal life given to believers.

For this the Lamb gave his life.

Leviticus 1:10–13
Isaiah 53:7
John 1:29, 1:36, 6:35–65, 13:1–35
Revelation 5:6–14, 14:1–5

Self-examination precedes partaking of the bread and wine,
in the light of the Scripture finding increased evidence of imputed holiness:
in personal commitment,
in family solidarity,
in educational obligations,
and in ecclesiastical responsibility,
together to push onwards in sanctification.

1 Corinthians 5:6–8, 11:27–32
1 Peter 1:18–19

55

24

In each congregation and throughout the Church,
vigor in sanctification appears in mutual discipline.

Leviticus 24:10–23; Numbers 15:32–36
Proverbs 17:17, 27:17
Matthew 18:15–20
1 Corinthians 5:1–5; Ephesians 4:1–16; 2 Timothy 3:1–9
Hebrews 10:19–25, 12:1–2
James 5:7–11
1 Peter 4:1–6

Communal love validates eschatological hope.

\\/

All members of each congregation,
beginning with the communicants,
assist the office bearers in sanctifying the congregation,
the men in the capacity of headship with the women helping.

Genesis 2:18
1 Corinthians 11:2–16; Galatians 5:7

Sinning within each communion and by the entire Church is intolerable.

Isaiah 48:9–11
Lamentation 3:31–33
1 Timothy 6:3–10

\\/

All hypocrisy and nominal membership must be rooted out of heart and hope.

Deuteronomy 9:4–12, 13:6–18, 17:2–7
1 Kings 13:18
Psalms 78:32–37, 119:120
Proverbs 30:12
Isaiah 43:22–24, 46:8–11, 50:10–11
Jeremiah 7:16–26, 12:2, 34:8–22
Ezekiel 33:30–33
Amos 5:21–24, 6:4–7
Micah 3:9–12
Haggai 1:7–11
Malachi 1:6–14, 2:13–16, 3:6–12
Matthew 6:1–4, 6:5–6, 7:1–5, 15:1–9, 16:24–28, 21:23–27, 23:1–39
Mark 7:1–13, 8:14–21, 11:27–33
Luke 6:46–49, 11:42–52, 12:41–48, 19:20–26, 22:1–8
Acts 15:1–5
Romans 2:1–11, 2:17–24; Colossians 2:16–19, 2:20–23; 1 Timothy 1:3–7; Titus 3:8–11
Hebrews 3:12–19, 13:9–10
James 1:5–8, 3:13–18
Revelation 2:13–17, 2:19–29

Duplicities of self-righteousness must give way to the fear of the Lord,
its accountability a joy.

Deuteronomy 4:9–14, 6:1–3, 10:12
1 Samuel 12:14, 12:24
Psalms 25:11–15, 33:18–19, 34:7–9, 34:11–14, 89:5–8, 111:9–10
Proverbs 1:7, 9:10, 14:27; Ecclesiastes 12:13–14
Isaiah 8:13, 29:13–14, 33:5–6
Jeremiah 2:19
2 Corinthians 5:11

All of Christ recognize that sins against the Holy Spirit lead into damnation,
its hellish fires fearsome.

Matthew 12:31–32, 13:49–50; Luke 12:10
Acts 5:1–11, 7:51–53, 11:1–18
Hebrews 6:1–8, 10:26–31
1 John 5:16–17
Revelation 14:17–20, 20:14–15

25

In the Church's eschatological journeying, the Lord Jesus draws many to himself;
always he imbues a remnant with wholeness.

Deuteronomy 33:26–29
1 Chronicles 16:13
Ezra 9:6–9
Isaiah 10:20–23, 46:3–4
Jeremiah 6:9; Lamentations 3:22–23
Ezekiel 11:13
Micah 2:12–13, 4:6–7, 5:7–9
Haggai 1:12–15
Zechariah 2:6–12
Malachi 1:2–4
Matthew 7:21–23, 11:25–30; Luke 10:21–22, 13:22–30, 14:15–24; John 6:37
Acts 1:15, 2:41
Romans 11:5; Ephesians 1:3–10
Revelation 7:4–8

Remnants he registered in the Book of Life,
reforming all as the light of the world.

Numbers 26:1–62
Matthew 5:14–16
Luke 10:20
Romans 8:28–30, 9:1—11:36
Revelation 20:12

All whom he gathers he holds in the light of holiness,
constantly cleansing and reforming.

Deuteronomy 26:16–19, 32:10–14
2 Chronicles 7:1–3
Psalm 5:11–12

Ecclesiastes 12:11–12
Matthew 19:16–22; Mark 13:24–27; John 6:37, 6:44, 15:16, 15:19
Romans 12:9–13; Ephesians 1:11–14; Colossians 3:1–4; 2 Thessalonians 2:13–15; 2
Timothy 2:19
Hebrews 3:7–11/Psalm 95:8–11; Hebrews 12:5–6/Proverbs 3:11–12
2 Peter 2:4–10

All others he bypasses;
these prove, by life-long sinning, the justice of reprobation.

Psalms 5:9–10, 73:15–20
Isaiah 6:9–10
Luke 20:18
Acts 28:25–28
Romans 9:32–33; 2 Thessalonians 2:11–12; 1 Timothy 1:19–20, 4:1–5, 5:24–25; 2
Timothy 2:16–18
Hebrews 4:1–7
1 John 2:18–25
Revelation 9:1–8

For this holiness he preserves, in every generation of the Church, a remnant,
a people holy to him and qualified by grace to will and to live the typically
Christian love.

Deuteronomy 33:29
Psalms 33:20–22, 100:1–5
Isaiah 10:20–23, 11:11, 28:5–6, 41:8–10
Haggai 1:14–15
John 15:18–25

Each remnant by way of the dividing-line,
the LORD separates to himself,
giving each a new name.

Genesis 17:5, 17:15, 32:28
2 Peter 1:3–22
Revelation 2:17, 3:12

26

Christy Jesus heart-holds the Church in holiness;
from out of the trinitarian union the Son affirms her consecration.
As she travels into the Eschaton he cleanses and reforms her.
By removing every trace of covetousness he recreates his own.

Psalm 93:5
Proverbs 9:1–6
Hosea 14:4–9
Joel 3:18
Amos 9:11–15/Acts 15:16–17
Habakkuk 3:17–19
Zephaniah 3:11–20
Matthew 16:13–20; Mark 11:15–19
Acts 2:43–47
Romans 12:3–7; Ephesians 1:15–23, 3:20–21; 1 Timothy 3:14–16
Revelation 1:17–20

As in the Old Testament dispensation,
equally in the New,
he identifies the covenant community.

The Church is his Temple.

Exodus 25:40
1 Chronicles 28:11, 19
Ezekiel 40:1—48:35
1 Corinthians 3:16–17

The Church is his Bride.

Isaiah 61:10–11
Ephesians 5:32–33
Revelation 19:6–8, 21:1–4

The Church is his Body.

Romans 12:3–8
1 Corinthians 12:12–31

The Church is his Flock.

Psalm 80:1a
Isaiah 40:11
Jeremiah 31:10–14
Matthew 9:36, 10:6, 26:31; John 10:11, 21:15–19
Hebrews 13:20
1 Peter 5:2

The Church is his Army.

Genesis 32:1–2
Joshua 5:13–15
1 Samuel 7:10, 17:26, 17:36, 17:45, 17:47
Psalm 2:1–11
Revelation 19:11–16

The Church is our Mother.*

Galatian 4.26

\/

In church renewal, his people look to him for more evidence of salvation:

relative to life,

Genesis 15:12–15
Jeremiah 31:27–28
Ezekiel 37:1–14
Matthew 19:16–22; Luke 10:25–28, 23:43

relative to food,

Exodus 15:24–25, 16:13–25
Psalms 78:15–16, 78:21–31, 104:27–30, 136:23–25, 144:12–15
Matthew 14:13–21, 15:32–39; Mark 6:30–44, 8:1–10; Luke 9:10–17;
John 6:1–14, 21:4–14
Revelation 22:1–5

and relative to the space of the covenant.

Exodus 3:7-8; Deuteronomy 34:4
Isaiah 54:1–3
Romans 4:13–15/Genesis 17:8

The Lord Jesus gathers the evidence of eternal life for his people.

Psalm 12:6
Isaiah 59:21
Jeremiah 31:31–34
Ezekiel 11:17–21, 36:22–32
John 3:16–17, 3:31–36, 5:24, 6:25–34, 6:68–69, 10:27–28, 12:25, 17:1–5

------

*The Church as Jesus's mother.

Revelation 12:1–6

27

With the Father and by the Spirit the Son in holiness created the heavens
and the earth,
the whole his universal rule,
the Earth his global Kingdom.

Psalms 19:1–6, 24:1–2, 145:10–13
Matthew 13:24–33, 13:44–50, 19:13–15, 19:23–30, 20:20–28
Mark 1:14–15, 4:26–32, 10:23–31
Luke 11:20, 13:18–21, 17:20–21, 18:15–17
Romans 14:17–18

At the heart of the Kingdom the Lord Jesus placed the Church.

Numbers 2:1–34
Matthew 16:13–20; Mark 8:27–30; Luke 9:18–22; John 6:67–69
Ephesians 1:15–23; Colossians 1:15–20; 1 Timothy 3:14–16

As the omnipotent Lord Jesus—by fiat—revealed the first creation;
over six days he created all,
from the farthest circling galaxy to the minutest spinning photon.

Genesis 1:1–31
Job 38:4–7
Psalms 33:6–7, 104:5–9
Proverbs 8:22–31
Isaiah 40:25–26
John 1:1–4
1 Corinthians 8:4–6; Colossians 1:15–16
Hebrews 1:10, 2:10

\/

After the Fall,

beginning in the Church,
Jesus recreated the eschatological Kingdom rooted in the Old Testament.*

2 Samuel 8:15–18
Deuteronomy 2:34–35
Isaiah 65:17–25
Ezekiel 37:1–14
Zephaniah 3:14–20
Matthew 12:22–30, 18:1–6

Now comes the Recreation,
the wholeness of the new heavens and earth:
Such is the power of the proclaimed Word.

Matthew 19:28
Romans 8:18–25, 10:14–17; 2 Corinthians 5:17; Ephesians 2:11–22, 4:22–24; Colossians 3:10
1 Peter 1:10–11, 1:22–24
Revelation 1:6, 11:15

As the resurrected and ascended Lord seated at the right hand of the
Father,
Jesus sanctifies the Church,
the heart of the Recreation.
From out of the Church he opens the heavens to his own.

Psalms 21:1–13, 99:1–5, 111:2–4
Ezekiel 40:1—48:35
John 14:1–7
1 Thessalonians 4:13–18
Hebrews 3:1–6
1 Peter 1:3–5
Revelation 1:12–16, 4:1—5:14, 21:1—22:21

------

*The LORD summoned David to reinitiate the Kingdom.

2 Samuel 7:10–11
Psalms 20:6, 89:1–4, 132:11–12
Matthew 1:1
Acts 15:16–17
Romans 1:3

THE RECREATED TIME

28

In the beginning the LORD, by dividing the light and the dark, created
time,
day and night,
each cycle measurable in twenty-four equal units.

Genesis 1:3–5

In the moving of the days,
today,
believers redeem the time,
persevering.

Psalms 31:15a, 39:4–6
Ephesians 5:16; Colossians 4:5
Hebrews 11:1–40
1 Peter 4:7
Revelation 14:12, 20:2

They who take history's off-ramps slowly fade into circularities,
carrying within them creative destruction.

Isaiah 40:21–24
Romans 13:11–14
Revelation 12:12

To know one's place in time and history relative to the Christ's Return
excites consecration.

Job 7:7
Psalms 39:11, 144:4
Ecclesiastes 3:1–9
Isaiah 64:1–3
Daniel 10:10–14, 11:2–45
Matthew 24:14; Mark 13:13; Luke 21:29–33
Romans 8:31–39; 1 Corinthians 7:31b; 2 Corinthians 6:2; Galatians 5:7; 1 Thessalo-
nians 5:1–11
Hebrews 6:1–8
1 Peter 1:13; 2 Peter 3:8–10

V

Persecution always threatens the Church,
if not from the inside then from the outside.

Mark 13:9–13; John 15:18
Acts 8:1–3, 9:1–9, 13:48–52, 14:19–23, 17:5–9, 21:7–14, 23:12–15
Romans 12:14–21; Galatians 4:28–31; 2 Thessalonians 1:5–12; 2 Timothy 2:11–13,
3:12–13
Hebrews 2:10–18, 11:32–38
1 Peter 3:13–22
Revelation 2:9–11

Paul's persecutions and sufferings are evidence.

Acts 8:1, 9:1–9, 22:20, 26:9–11
Galatians 1:13–14; 1 Timothy 1:12–14

29

Over days, weeks, years, centuries, and millennia the Lord Jesus,
sovereign and omnipotent,
creates history every day.

Daily he lays down the route for the Church's gratitude.

Genesis 50:20; Leviticus 26:1–13; Deuteronomy 5:6–21, 28:1–14
Joshua 24:1–13
Ruth 4:18–22
Esther 9:1–15
Luke 1:14–17, 1:32–33
Romans 15:21; Ephesians 2:10
2 Peter 3:11–13

In and with the Scriptures the Lord Jesus gave knowledge of the past,
therewith in the present to interpret the future.

Romans 13:11–14; 2 Corinthians 4:16–18
Hebrews 12:25–29
1 Peter 4:7–11, 5:10
1 John 2:7–11, 2:18–25
Revelation 1:7, 6:9–11

\/

Covetous peoples and empires,
reactionary in being and ignorant of the common good,
walk away from the main route and seek histories at variance to Jesus's
lordship.

Exodus 10:1–2
Esther 3:7–15
Jeremiah 18:15, 23:12

Matthew 6:32–33; Luke 12:27–31
I Thessalonians 5:1–3

Off the main road these engage unforgiveable sins.

Matthew 12:31–32; Mark 3:28–30, 9:42–50; Luke 12:8–12
Hebrews 6:4–8
James 1:13–15
2 Peter 3:15–16
1 John 5:16b

\/

Jesus,
the LORD God,
from out of the first dispensation alerted the Church to sinning's conse-
quences.

Leviticus 26:14–39; Deuteronomy 28:15–68

In cleansing the world he warned the nations to beware.

Psalms 2:1–11, 22:27–28, 33:10–12, 37:20
Isaiah 13:1–8, 13:9–16
Jeremiah 18:1–11, 19:1–15, 25:15–16
Joel 3:9–21
Amos 1:1—2:16, 4:6–13
Micah 7:11–13, 7:16–17
Zephaniah 2:1–15, 3:8–10
Zechariah 9:1–8
Romans 1:18–23, 1:24–25
Revelation 10:11, 12:7–12, 14:6–8, 14:9–11, 16:16, 20:11–15

In the BC and AD millennia,
Jesus locates the Church on her way to the Eschaton.

The Church is basic to the times;
in her—shepherd-wise*—Jesus enfolds his own and for her structures
history.

Psalms 93:1–2, 100:3
Isaiah 40:9–11
Micah 5:2–4, 7:14
John 10:10b–11
Acts 20:28–31

Hebrews 12:18–24
1 Peter 5:2–3
Revelation 7:1–8, 14:1–5

In the Church he begins the Judgment,
to demonstrate universally and historically the fairness of divine justice.

Psalms 34:16, 98:7–9
Isaiah 63:3–9
Amos 7:7–9
John 9:39
Acts 17:30–31
James 5:9
1 Peter 4:17

------

*Bad shepherds are warned.

Jeremiah 23:1–4
Ezekiel 34:1–31
Zechariah 10:3–5, 11:4–6, 13:7–9
John 10:13

30

Over millennia sinfulness penetrated the created order.
The Lord Jesus, however, preserved the whole,
the Earth specifically,
for the sake of the Church and for the coming of the Kingdom.

Genesis 9:12–17

\/

To beat down evils attacking the Church he reveals his wrath.

In the first dispensation he sent sword, pestilence, and famine.

Deuteronomy 7:17–26
2 Samuel 21:1
1 Kings 8:37–40; 2 Kings 8:1–3
Psalm 11:6
Isaiah 24:1–23, 26:21, 66:6, 66:15–16
Jeremiah 14:11–12, 15:2, 24:10
Ezekiel 7:1–9
Joel 1:4–12
Amos 3:13–15, 4:4–12, 9:5–8, 9:9–10
Obadiah 1–21
Micah 1:2–7
Nahum 1:1—3:9, 3:19
Habakkuk 2:15–17, 3:1–16
Haggai 2:15–19
Zechariah 5:1–4

In the second dispensation he sends calamities.

Matthew 24:1–44; Mark 13:1–36; Luke 21:5–28
Acts 2:19–21

Revelation 6:1–17, 7:1–17, 8:1–13, 9:1–21, 16:1–21, 19:17–21

Thus he initiates the punishment of unbelievers.

Deuteronomy 6:16–19, 9:4–5
1 Samuel 2:10a
Psalms 22:29–31, 55:9–11, 92:5–9
Matthew 11:20–24, 12:38–42; Luke 10:13–15
2 Timothy 3:1–9

Thus also he tests believers' faithfulness.

Psalms 11:4, 66:8–12, 78:41, 78:56–57, 139:19–20
Isaiah 3:13–15
1 Corinthians 10:6–13; 2 Corinthians 9:13–14, 13:5–10; Galatians 6:1–5; Philippians
4:10–16
Hebrews 10:32–36, 12:5–6
James 1:2–4, 1:12–15

\/

As the Son of Man he wills accountability first from office bearers.

Psalm 8:3–4
Ezekiel 2:1–7
Daniel 7:13 14
Matthew 9:1–8, 11:19, 12:8, 16:13–20, 26:64
Mark 8:31–33, 9:9–13, 9:30–32, 10:32–34, 13:26, 14:21, 14:62
Luke 5:24, 9:22, 9:26, 12:8–12, 17:22–27, 18:8, 18:31–34, 19:10
John 1:51, 5:22–23, 5:26–27, 6:62, 8:28, 9:35, 12:23, 12:34, 13:31–32
Acts 7:56
Revelation 14:14–16

\/

By manifesting his people in holiness,
sanctifying all,
he reveals the centrality of the Church,
the Kingdom,
and the salvation of his people.

Hence he provides for his people.

Exodus 16:13–21; Numbers 13:25–27, 21:16–18; Deuteronomy 7:12–16, 8:1–10,
12:20–28

Joshua 5:10–12, 23:14–16
1 Kings 4:20, 4:25
Psalms 67:1–6, 84:5–6
Isaiah 30:23–26
Joel 2:23–29
Zechariah 10:1
Matthew 14:13–21, 15:32–39; Mark 6:37–44; Luke 12:22–31

THE RECREATED PENITENCE

31

For purifying the Church, Christ Jesus commanded all to trinitarian prayer.

True to his pardoning work God the Son hears penitential prayer.

Exodus 2:23–25
1 Kings 8:33–34
Psalms 32:3–5, 44:23–26, 65:1–4, 79:8–10, 130:7–8, 145:8–9
Isaiah 58:1–5
Jeremiah 4:1–4, 4:14, 14:7, 25:1–7
Joel 2:12–14
Micah 7:18–20
Matthew 7:7, 9:13; Luke 5:32
1 Timothy 1:15
1 John 1:5–10, 5:14

Due to Jesus's atoning work the God the Father hears penitential prayer.

Matt 6:7–13; Luke 11:1–4
Mathew 6:6, 6:14–15; John 14:6, 14:13, 15:16, 16:23–24

Through Jesus's atoning work the Holy Spirit leads in prayer.

Romans 8:12–17, 8:26–27
Ephesians 6:18–20
Jude 20

In the humility of penitence believers submit to the pain of repentance, confessing the upwelling Adamic sin.

*For godly grief produces a repentance that leads to salvation and brings no
regret,
but worldly grief produces death.*

Exodus 9:27
Jeremiah 2:26–28
Matthew 26:41
2 Corinthians 7:10
Revelation 3:18–19

In the freedom and cleanliness of holiness believers lay out before the
Judge
all cruxes of covetousness and hearts of sinfulness;
they do so communally and personally.

John 8:36
Galatians 5:1–12, 5:17

In the Father and with the Spirit Jesus upheld the trinitarian bond for
praying.

32

At the command of the Lord and Savior believers humbly bow also before
the Father,
confessing covetousness with respect to the Kingdom.

\/

Every image bearer who seeks to own (parts of) the Kingdom
—an empire, a country, a business, a property—
finds perverse glories.

Genesis 13:10–11, 25:29–34
2 Kings 18:28–35
Daniel 4:29–30, 5:2–4
Matthew 19:16–22, 20:20–21, 21:12–13
Luke 12:16–21, 15:11–13, 16:14–15, 16:19–31, 22:3–6

Such image bearers sooner or later stand before the Lord,
fully accountable.

\/

All in Christ Jesus renounce this perversion of the image of God.
He wills to break such hardness of heart.

Psalms 9:5–6, 66:18–19
Isaiah 59:1–2
Haggai 1:1–6
Malachi 1:14
John 9:31
James 4:3
1 Peter 3:7

With his redemptive work—Mark 1:14–15—Jesus reclaimed the

Kingdom;
he sanctifies his people for the Father.
In the Lord's reign—evidence of holiness—every form of ownership serves
one goal,
by the image of God to manage (parts of) the Kingdom,
every proprietary interest stripped even of covetous taints.

Genesis 12:1
Leviticus 25:8–22; Deuteronomy 15:11
Psalms 8:1–9, 41:1
Isaiah 25:4
Jeremiah 22:16
2 Corinthians 8:1–7, 9:6–14

Through ownership covenantally recreated,
believers in prayer confess improper interests in (parts of) the Kingdom,
thus to sacrifice every property to the Father and the Son in the Spirit.

Exodus 23:10–11, 25:1–9
Judges 6:25–27
Matthew 17:24–27, 18:23–35, 22:15–22; Luke 3:10–14

33

The Church at prayer easily submits to the divine will,
always only to walk by the Spirit.

\\/

In Christ believers confess every travesty of willing,
never again to gratify its demands.

Proverbs 19:21
Matthew 6:10b, 7:21–23, 12:46–50; Mark 3:31–35; Luke 8:19–21
Romans 7:13–20; Galatians 5:16; Ephesians 4:15–16, 5:17
1 Peter 4:1–2
1 John 2:17

Nevertheless, believers en route wage tiresome skirmishes,
the human will against the divine.
The human will is powerful in its familiarity.

Exodus 5:20–21, 14:10–12; Numbers 14:1–3
Psalm 7:12–16
Matthew 6:2–4, 7:3–5, 7:21, 11:16–19, 15:8–9/Isaiah 29:13, 26:41
Philippians 3:17–21

Mercifully the divine will breaks down the covetousness of the human.
This dying and death hurts.
In each generation new creations appear in the light of holiness.

John 3:8
Romans 6:4, 8:10; 2 Corinthians 5:16–18

The persevering Church as one petitions:

Teach me to do your will,
for you are my God!

Psalms 40:8, 143:10a
Romans 14:19; 2 Corinthians 3:2–3

With the human will covenantally recreated,
believers in prayer sacrifice respective wills to the Father and the Son,
in the Spirit.

1 Kings 8:22–53
Matthew 16:24–26
Romans 12:1–2; 1 Corinthians 7:17–24; Ephesians 6:5–9; Philippians 4:8–9; Titus
2:11–14

34

From the beginning the LORD God provided his own with food.

Genesis 1:29, 3:19, 9:3

Throughout the first dispensation he provided the essentials,
leaving all unencumbered and free to serve him.

Exodus 16:13–21, 17:1–7; Leviticus 26:3–5; Numbers 11:31–35; Deuteronomy 8:3,
26:1–4, 26:12–15, 28:1–6
Joshua 5:10–12

In the second dispensation Jesus commands believers to petition also the
Father for sustenance.
This ordering of reality the Spirit presses home.
In the trinitarian manner God grants the recreated Church the necessities
—food, drink, clothing, shelter—
as he promised.

Matthew 6:11, 6:32, 10:10
Acts 2:43–47
1 Timothy 6:7–8

Such dependence upon the Father and the Son runs against the grain.
Trust in seasonal rains suits better.

Nevertheless by faith the Church attends to the sowing and harvesting,
rejoicing at every ingathering:

The earth has yielded its increase;
God, our God, has blessed us.

Psalms 65:9–13, 67:1–6

With the essentials covenantally promised, believers cleanse each congregation and heart of covetous spirits.

Romans 14:1–9

35

At the command of the Christ:
Believers burdened by injustice(s) seek justice from him and the Father,
trusting that the Father and the Son are eminently qualified to invoke
righteousness.

Beloved,
never avenge yourselves,
but leave it to the wrath of God,
for it is written,
"Vengeance is mine,
I will repay,
says the Lord."

Leviticus 19:18
1 Kings 8:31–32; 2 Kings 13:4, 19:35–37
Psalms 12:7–8, 37:1–4, 37:5–6, 55:22
Matthew 5:38–42, 5:43–48
Romans 12:19; 1 Corinthians 4:11–13
Hebrews 10:30
1 Peter 2:23

Still, in the Church, yearnings for retribution endure.

Genesis 27:41
2 Samuel 3:26–30, 13:23–29
Luke 9:51–56, 13:6–9, 22:49

Believers now put to death this perversion of the image of God in them.
With justice covenantally recreated,
all in Christ prayerfully leave retaliatory satisfactions to the Father and to
the Son.

In fact,
believers set the norm for pardoning,

. . . forgive us our debts,
as we have forgiven our debtors.

Matthew 6:14–15, 7:12, 18:21–35
Luke 6:31

For this, Jesus set the standard.

Mark 11:25; Luke 7:36–50
Romans 15:1–6; 2 Corinthians 2:5–11

36

The Lord Jesus's command stands firm:

He and the Father forbid coveting all seductions of the darkness.

Genesis 13:10–11, 19:26, 38:15–18
Deuteronomy 5:21, 7:25
1 Samuel 30:22; 2 Samuel 12:1–6, 15:1–6, 24:1–4
2 Kings 5:19–27
Micah 2:2
Haggai 1:1–6
James 4:2

In prayer all in the Church ask that in the Spirit they may remain strong,
to prevent defeat in sin and shaming the Father and the Son.

All journeying into the Eschaton seek fortification against all enemies,
Satan's fiery arrows specifically.

Psalms 25:2, 53:5
Acts 7:52
Ephesians 6:16
1 Peter 5:6–11

No temptation has overtaken you that is not common to man.
God is faithful, and he will not let you be tempted beyond your ability,
but with the temptation he will also provide the way of escape,
that you may be able to endure it.

1 Corinthians 10:13
James 1:13–14

With conquering power covenantally recreated,
all in Christ prayerfully overcome and destroy temptation.

Ezra 9:6–15
Nehemiah 1:4–11, 9:6–38
Matthew 6:13, 26:41
1 Corinthians 7:5; 1 Timothy 6:9

37

It is the will of the Lord Jesus that his people cease coveting (parts of) the
Kingdom,
craving its power and its glory.

Satan and his pretend they own the Lord's radiant dominion.

Numbers 14:4–10; Deuteronomy 8:11–20
Isaiah 14:12–21
Ezekiel 28:1–10
Daniel 4:10–12
Matthew 4:8–10, 10:39, 19:23–24; Luke 4:5–7; 12:13–21

Bartering lives for a dust mote of the Kingdom appeals.

Matt 16:24–26; Luke 14:27

Better is a handful of quietness than two hands full of toil and a striving
after wind.

Psalm 90:13–17
Ecclesiastes 4:6
Philippians 3:8
1 Timothy 6:6–8, 6:17–19

Aggressive and passive human capacities to own the Father and the Son's
world,
whatever the damages socially and ecologically,
find the shame of destitution.

Psalms 73:16–17, 74:9–11
Joel 2:20
Amos 4:10
Luke 16:19–31

1 Timothy 6:10
Hebrews 13:5
Revelation 11:18p, 20:1–3

With ownership of the Kingdom in holy hands,
believers in prayer denounce boundless cravings.

Philippians 3:12–16

38

All in real amendment know the pain of repentance;
each repudiates satisfactions of hypocrisy.

Numbers 12:9–16, 14:17–19, 21:7–9
Nehemiah 8:11, 9:1–3
Psalms 34:15–18, 34:19–22, 51:3–9
Ezekiel 20:1–8
Micah 6:6–8
Luke 18:9–14

Believers therefore in the Spirit validate the holiness welling up from
within hearts of flesh.

Psalm 77:13
Ezekiel 36:22–32
John 6:63
Acts 20:24
Romans 8:12–13; 1 Corinthians 3:1–4; Galatians 5:19; Philippians 3:8–9; Colossians
3:5

Your decrees are very trustworthy;
holiness befits your house,
O LORD,
forevermore.

Leviticus 4:1–35
Psalms 19:11–13, 20:6, 93:5
1 Thessalonians 3:11–13

Jesus taught that no matter how often one (an individual, a congregation,
the Church) sins he,
the Savior,
hears genuine repentance and, in oneness with the Father, forgives.

Psalm 78:38–39
Isaiah 43:25–28, 48:17–19, 59:16–20
Jeremiah 3:11–18, 3:24–25
Matthew 18:21–35
James 5:16

At issue is not the divine readiness to remit sins,
but believers' willingness and ability to repent.

Matthew 6:14–15

Out of love for the Lord Jesus and the Father,
all of the Church, in consecration, engage the Ten Commandments.

Romans 12:1–2; Colossians 2:8–15

Members of Christ orient inner and outer selves,
as does each congregation,
to that which glories in the eschatological future.

THE RECREATED GRATITUDE

39

Gratitude runs forever,
glorifying the Trinity into all eternity.

Exodus 19:18–20, 20:1–17, 32:15–16; Leviticus 18:1–5, 26:13, 26:46; Deuteronomy
5:6–21, 6:1–3, 7:1–5, 10:1–5
Hosea 6:6
Malachi 4:4

Beginning here and now in the sanctifying way the powers of grace bear
fruit.
All in every congregation walk in the light of holiness,
thoughts, words, and deeds expressive of the love of the Lord,
grateful in the fear of the Lord for the accountability.

Deuteronomy 32:44–47
Psalms 19:7–10, 36:1–12, 97:11–12, 119:1–176
2 Corinthians 10:5–6; Galatians 3:23–29
Hebrews 8:8–12

Hence,

To the teaching and to the testimony!

Isaiah 1:18–20, 8:20a
James 1:22

Christ Jesus, by the imposition of the Law, forms and reforms consciences,
until all his abide by the same ethical standard.*

Psalm 103:15–18
Proverbs 28:9
Matthew 5:17–20; Luke 16:16–17
James 2:8–13

Hence, again,
gratitude in good works opens up holiness in righteousness.

Matthew 5:14–16; John 14:21
Romans 13:8–10; 1 Corinthians 6:9–11, 7:17; Colossians 2:6, 3:12–17

The way of gratitude starts in the Church, always.

Isaiah 35:8, 40:3–5, 43:14–21, 49:8–23, 62:10–12
Acts 9:2, 19:23, 22:4, 24:22

------

*The Law also exposes sin, apparent ten times in the exposition of the
Commandments.

40

The Lord Jesus tolerates gods neither next to him nor to the Father and
the Spirit;
displacement of the Persons of the Trinity garners his wrath.

Exodus 32:7–8; Deuteronomy 4:15–24, 4:32–40, 16:21–22
Joshua 23:6–11
1 Corinthians 8:4–6, 10:14–22

The I AM wills all honor for the Three-in-One of whom he is one.

Exodus 22:20, 23:23–25; Numbers 25:1–5; Deuteronomy 10:1–5
Psalms 81:6–10, 96:1–6, 97:6–9
Isaiah 65:1–7
Matthew 4:10; Luke 4:8
1 Corinthians 10:6–13
1 John 5:21

Yet religiosities, sects,* and cults** push the Persons of the Trinity aside,
covetously to claim a prohibited glory,
self-justification.

Exodus 34:11–17; Deuteronomy 9:13–21, 12:1–4, 12:29–31, 32:15–18, 32:19–22
1 Kings 11:1–8, 12:28, 14:23–24
Isaiah 2:12–19

All idolatries face a grievous future,
condemnation sure;
moreover idolaters become what they worship.

Leviticus 18:21, 19:4, 19:31, 20:1–5, 20:6–9, 20:27, 26:1–2; Deuteronomy 4:25–31,
27:15
Judges 2:1–5
1 Samuel 15:23a

2 Kings 10:18–27, 17:7–18, 23:26–27
1 Chronicles 9:1b, 16:26
Psalms 115:3–8, 135:15–18
Romans 1:18–23, 1:24–25; 1 Corinthians 6:9–11
Revelation 19:1–6

Beginning in the Church, hatred for idolatry gathers strength.

Psalm 16:4
Isaiah 41:5–7, 44:9–20, 46:5–7, 66:17, 66:24
Jeremiah 2:9–13, 3:6–10, 7:30–34, 8:1–3, 23:12–15, 23:16–17
Ezekiel 8:7–13
Daniel 3:1–30, 4:1–37
Hosea 2:1–13, 5:5–7
Habakkuk 2:18–19
Zephaniah 1:2–6
Zechariah 1:1–6, 3:1–5
1 Corinthians 12:1–3

------

    *Sect: a schismatic break to pioneer a more than holy church formation.
**Cult: an enforcement of a religious idea, its leader(s) recruiting followers from the Church.

41

Even as denominations schismatically multiply the Lord Jesus wills con-
cord in worship;
as the Head of the Church he is the Liturgist and the Exegete who unifies
the worshiping Church.

Psalms 95:1–5
John 17:6–19
1 Corinthians 1:10, 14:33
Revelation 1:12–16

Jesus, according to his will, instituted the acceptable way of worship;
none dare with substitutions and devices of human imaginations to per-
vert liturgies
—much by less Satan's suggestions—
to remove attention from the proclamation of the Word.

Deuteronomy 12:5–7, 12:10–14
1 Kings 12:25–33
Isaiah 1:12–17
Habakkuk 2:20
Matthew 4:10; Luke 4:8; John 4:23–24
1 Corinthians 11:2–16, 14:33–36

Communal worship centers on reading the Scriptures and the proclamation of the Word.*

Exodus 25:1—31:18, 35:1—40:38
1 Kings 6:1–38; 2 Kings 12:9–16
2 Chronicles 29:3–36
Ezra 6:13–18
Nehemiah 10:32–39
Ezekiel 40:1—48:35

They who break up the Body, the Bride, the Flock, and the Army of the
Christ,
to idolize inventions and projections of the imagination,
find that beginning in the Church Jesus wills worship without compro-
mise and hypocrisy.

Exodus 32:1–6; Deuteronomy 12:8–9
2 Timothy 2:8–14
Hebrews 12:18–24

Fathers, son(s), grandson(s), and great-grandson(s) who disbelieve the
Christ's headship,
covetously moved,
discover the fierceness of his wrath to the third and fourth generation;
they also simultaneously experience the social costs.

Exodus 34:6–7, 34:14; Deuteronomy 7:9–10
Isaiah 45:22–23, 48:1–2, 55:1–2, 66:22–23
Luke 1:11–12
John 4:23–24
Ephesians 6:4; Colossians 3:21
Hebrews 12:29/Deuteronomy 4:24

----

*Acceptable congregational worship includes teaching, admonishment,
psalm/hymn singing, prayer, and sacramental observances with thanksgiv-
ing and in humbleness.

42

As the Church breaks down, blasphemy rages,
accompanied by foul language.

Matthew 12:24–28; Mark 3:22–27; Luke 11:15–20
1 Corinthians 12:1–3; Ephesians 5:4; Colossians 3:8
James 3:9–10

Blasphemers consistently despise the Persons of the Trinity,
coveting the downfall of the Son, of the Father, and of the Spirit.

Exodus 22:28; Leviticus 24:10–23
Matthew 27:39–44; Mark 15:17–20, 15:29–32; Luke 23:35–37; John 19:3

Hence,
in the Church,
the more members push the Name asunder the worse the profanities.

Leviticus 5:4; Numbers 14:15–16
Job 2:9
Ezekiel 36:20–21; 39:7–8
Amos 8:11–12
Romans 3:14

\\/

All who are in Christ Jesus reverently and humbly uphold the trinitarian
names.

Job 1:5
Romans 16:25–27; 2 Corinthians 13:11–14; Galatians 3:1–5; 2 Timothy 1:8–10

Everywhere and in all situations the people of the Lord,

beginning in the holiness of worship,
utter the divine names with reverence.

*Shout, and sing for joy, O inhabitants of Zion,
for great in your midst is the Holy One of Israel.*

Isaiah 12:6

By calling upon the name of the Lord, oaths carry weights of integrity.

Genesis 24:3
Joshua 2:12–14, 9:18
Matthew 5:33–37
Hebrews 6:13
James 5:12

43

With covetously pursued labors, pleasures, and "good" causes,
idolizing spirits erode the worth of sabbath rest;
blending these by enculturation into evil is to worship other gods,
the social costs of which immense.

Numbers 15:32–36
Nehemiah 13:15–18
Isaiah 58:13–14

\/

In the first dispensation the covenant people rested each Seventh Day,
to know themselves in the glory of divine holiness and in the fear of the
Lord.
In the second dispensation, on First Days, Christ's members called together
—to know themselves in the divine holiness of the eternal sabbath—
rest in the fear of the Lord preparatory to the week ahead,
thus generating sanctification.

Leviticus 19:30
Nehemiah 13:19–22

These are the primary days for the Word.

Isaiah 55:6–9, 56:6–8, 66:22–23
Jeremiah 17:19–27
Matthew 12:1–8; Mark 2:23–28, 3:1–6; Luke 13:10–17, 14:1–4; John 5:10–18,
7:21–22, 9:13–14
Revelation 1:10

In these days of rest, all in Christ gather for inspiration by the love of God.

Exodus 23:12–17, 34:21, 35:1–3

On the Seventh Day in the Old Testament the Lord's people listened to
him.
On First Days in the second dispensation they hear him.
They integrate the Fourth Commandment into the holiness of the Church,
celibacy, marriage, families, education, work, and even recreation.

44

By disparagement of the Scriptures and with rising individualism,
each person covetously becomes a decisive authority.
This is the perceived norm.

\/

For the consecration of each congregation, the Lord Jesus commands:

children to honor parents

Exodus 12:26–27 21:15, 21:17; Leviticus 19:3; Deuteronomy 21:18–21, 27:16
Joshua 4:21
Psalm 144:12
Proverbs 1:8, 4:1, 10:1, 19:13, 20:20, 23:22
Matthew 21:28–31
Ephesians 6:1–3; Colossians 3:20

parents to honor the Lord

Psalms 22:4, 78:1–8, 127:3–5, 128:1–8

office bearers to honor the Office Bearer.

Matthew 18:1–5; Mark 9:36–37
1 Timothy 5:17
Hebrews 13:7

\/

Beginning in the Church the norms for authority stand out clearly:

for parents and teachers

Psalm 78:1–4
Ephesians 6:4; Colossians 3:21
James 3:1–5

for office bearers

Matthew 21:23–27
I Timothy 3:1–13
1 Peter 5:1–5

for governments, courts, and police

Numbers 12:1–16, 16:1–50
Matthew 22:15–22
Romans 13:1–7
1 Peter 2:13–17

All in all,

. . . [submit] to one another out of reverence for Christ.

Ephesians 5:21

The Lord God prohibits treason.

2 Samuel 15:13–18, 20:1–2
1 Kings 1:9–10

45

The Lord Jesus created life and upholds the first covenant promise.

Genesis 18:9–15
Psalm 139:13–18
Matthew 10:39, 16:24–25; Luke 1:14–17, 17:33; John 1:4, 5:21, 5:25, 6:35, 11:25,
12:25, 17:3
2 Corinthian 5:4; Colossians 3:4
Revelation 2:7, 22:1–2

Where Christianity fades, neighbors' lives cheapen;
then covetous forces, huge with collateral damages, assume control.

War

Genesis 14:1–12
Joshua 9:1–2, 10:1–21, 11:1–15
Judges 4:12–16, 9:42–49
1 Samuel 17:1–11, 29:1–5; 2 Samuel 8:1–14, 18:1–15
1 Kings 8:33–34, 20:26–30; 2 Kings 19:35–37
Psalm 46:6

Homicide

Genesis 4:8, 9:6
Exodus 2:11–15; Deuteronomy 19:11–13, 27:24–25
1 Samuel 22:11–19; 2 Samuel 1:15; 2 Samuel 2:23, 3:27, 4:7, 11:14–17, 13:23–29,
18:14–15, 20:10a
Matthew 5:21–26

Abortion   Eugenics   Euthanasia

Suicide

1 Samuel 31:4–5; 2 Samuel 17:23
1 Kings 16:18–19
Matthew 27:5/Acts 1:18–19

Carelessness

Exodus 21:12–14; Numbers 35:9–14; Deuteronomy 19:1–10

Cannibalism

1 Kings 3:16–22; 2 Kings 6:28–31
Ezekiel 5:10

Substance Abuse

Genesis 9:20–21
1 Samuel 25:36–38
Isaiah 28:7–8
Jeremiah 13:12–14
Daniel 5:2–4
Amos 4:1–3

Hatred

Proverbs 14:30
Matthew 5:21–26
Romans 1:29, 12:19; Galatians 5:19–21; 2 Timothy 3:1–5
James 1:20
1 John 2:9–11, 3:15

Pollution

Isaiah 10:15–19
Revelation 6:1–17, 8:1—9:21, 14:17–20, 16:1–24

\/

Beginning in the Church, sanctification holds neighbors high.

Exodus 23:4
Matthew 5:5, 5:43–48, 7:12, 22:39; Luke 6:36
Romans 12:9–13, 12:18, 12:20, 13:8–10; Galatians 6:1–2; Ephesians 4:1–3; Philippians 2:1–4
1 Peter 3:8

They who disparage neighbors' lives show, thereby, the condemnation they face.

1 John 2:9, 2:11

103

46

From the beginning,
the Lord God and Almighty Creator ordered the man-woman bond and
aligned sexuality;
with clarity he defined the genders.

Genesis 1:27, 2:21–25
Romans 7:1–3; 1 Corinthians 7:1–9, 7:39–40, 11:2–16; Ephesians 5:21–33; Colossians 3:18–25; 1 Timothy 2:8–15
Hebrews 13:4
1 Peter 3:1–7

He condemned extra-marital sexuality.
They who seek fornicative gratifications cause guilt and cost for themselves and others.

Homosexualism/Lesbianism

Genesis 19:4–5
Leviticus 18:22, 20:13; Deuteronomy 23:18
Judges 19:22
1 Kings 14:24, 15:12, 22:46
Romans 1:26–27; 1 Corinthians 6:9–11

Bestiality

Exodus 22:19; Leviticus 18:23, 20:15–16; Deuteronomy 27:21

Adultery

Genesis 16:1–6
Leviticus 18:20, 20:10; Deuteronomy 22:22
2 Samuel 3:7, 11:2–5, 16:20–22
Proverbs 6:32

Matthew 5:27–30

Divorce/Remarriage

Deuteronomy 24:1–4
Matthew 5:31–32, 19:3–9; Mark 6:17–19, 10:2–12; Luke 3:19–20, 16:18
Romans 7:1–3; 1 Corinthians 7:10–11, 7:15

Bisexualism

Deuteronomy 22:5

Pornography Surrogacy Cohabitation Transgenderism

Polygamy

Genesis 20:17, 28:6–9, 35:23–26
2 Samuel 5:13, 12:7–9, 16:20–23
Esther 2:12–14

Polyamory

Genesis 20:17–18
2 Samuel 3:2–5
1 Kings 11:1–8

Premarital Sex

Exodus 22:16–17; Deuteronomy 22:13–21, 22:28–29

Prostitution

Leviticus 19:29, 21:9; Deuteronomy 22:20–21, 23:17–18
Hosea 4:13b–14
1 Corinthians 6:12–20

Incest

Genesis 19:30-38, 20:2, 20:12, 35:22, 49:4
Leviticus 18:6–18, 20:17–22; Deuteronomy 27:22–23
2 Samuel 3:6–11, 13:14, 16:20–23
Ezekiel 22:10–11
1 Corinthians 5:1–5

(Statutory) Rape

Genesis 34:1–7
Leviticus 19:20–22; Deuteronomy 22:23–29
2 Samuel 13:14

Bigamy

Genesis 4:23–24, 16:1–6, 44:23–24
Exodus 29:21–30; Leviticus 18:17, 20:14; Deuteronomy 21:15–17
1 Samuel 1:1–2, 25:43–44
Matthew 14:1–12; Mark 6:14–29

Exogamy/Intermarriage

Genesis 38:1–5; Deuteronomy 7:3–4
Joshua 23:12–13
Ezra 9:10–15, 10:1–5
Nehemiah 10:28–31, 13:23–27
2 Corinthians 6:14–7:1

Fornicative human beings find themselves in the fires of condemnation.

\/

In the Church, believers through sanctification create respect for and trust
in respective spouses,
to lead next generations to glorify the Lord in human sexuality for the
marriage of the future.

Genesis 2:24–25
1 Corinthians 7:1–7; 1 Thessalonians 4:1–8
Revelation 19:6–10

47

The Lord Jesus from the beginning established clear boundaries by dividing neighbors' goods.
All thievery he therefore hates.

Of money

Jeremiah 6:13–15, 8:8–13
John 12:6

Of goods

Leviticus 6:1–7, 19:11
Luke 12:41–48

Of fraud/identity theft

Leviticus 19:13, 19:35–36; Deuteronomy 19:14, 24:14–15, 25:13–16, 27:17
Joshua 9:1–27
Proverbs 11:1
Luke 19:1–10
Acts 5:1–11
1 Corinthians 6:7–8

Of usury

Exodus 22:25–27; Leviticus 25:35–38
Nehemiah 5:7
Psalm 15:5

Of robbery

Exodus 22:1–2
Proverbs 1:7–19

Of kidnapping/trafficking

Exodus 21:16; Deuteronomy 21:10–14, 24:7
Amos 2:6
1 Timothy 1:10

Of insider trading

Matthew 26:14–16; Mark 14:10–11; Luke 22:3–6; John 18:2–3

Of bribery

Exodus 23:6–8; Deuteronomy 10:17, 27:25
Isaiah 5:23
Amos 5:12
Acts 24:26

Beginning in the Church and in the sanctification of all justified by faith,
they who break the boundaries of ownership,
coveting what belongs to others,
experience in the end its terrible social shame.

Luke 16:19–31

Hence,
everyone in Christ Jesus serves the welfare of others,
with trust and respect building community.

2 Corinthians 4:16–18; Galatians 6:10; Ephesians 4:28

48

The Lord Jesus, beginning among his own, ordered his people to love, basic to which building up the reputations of others.

In court

Leviticus 5:1, 19:12, 19:15–16; Deuteronomy 19:15–21, 27:19
Proverbs 6:19, 14:5
1 Corinthians 6:1–8

In church

John 8:44, 8:55

In family situations

Exodus 21:17; Leviticus 19:3; Deuteronomy 27:16
Proverbs 4:24, 5:3, 6:12–15, 10:32, 19:1

In the neighborhood

Jeremiah 9:4–6
Ephesians 4:29

Also by way of social media.

He therefore condemns also the guilts and social costs of:

slander/gossip

Exodus 23:1–3, 23:6–8
Psalms 12:1–4, 12:3–4, 31:18, 37:12–13, 41:6–7, 64:1–6
Proverbs 7:1–20

Matthew 26:61, 27:40; Mark 14:57–58
James 4:6–12

bullying

1 Kings 21:8–14

scapegoating

Matthew 27:39–44; Mark 15:29–32; Luke 23:35–37; John 11:49–52, 18:14

Covetous abuse of others disparages the good names of neighbors.

All who are in Christ seek the wellbeing of neighbors as evidence of sanctification,
however strong temptations may be for verbal abuse.

Philippians 2:14–18; Colossians 4:5–6; 1 Thessalonians 3:11–13
James 1:19–21, 3:1–12, 4:11–12
1 Peter 3:8–12, 3:14–18

49

The Lord Jesus condemned every covetous action,
whether of heart, soul, mind, or hand,
for through the Adamic sin the Devil moves people to oppose the Christ
with ingratitude.

Genesis 13:11; Exodus 22:29; Numbers 14:20–25, 16:31–35
Ezra 4:1–3
Proverbs 6:16–19
Hosea 4:4–6
Micah 2:1–5, 6:9–14, 7:1–7
Haggai 1:1–6
Malachi 1:8
Matthew 20:20–28; Mark 10:35–45; Luke 9:46–48

Beginning in the Church, believers,
moved by the Word and the Spirit,
through sanctification cease giving in to covetousness.
Sins of opposing the Lord Jesus and harming neighbors bear condemnation.

Deuteronomy 11:18–25
Psalms 31:19–20, 37:10–11, 37:18–19
John 15:10
Ephesians 6:10–17; Philippians 1:6
Hebrews 12:12–17

Sins against the commandments are identifiable,
except for the Tenth.
Coveting is a matter of the heart where the Lord Jesus judges,
condemning even least traces of refusal and failure to respect the divine
will.

Psalms 10:10–11, 10:12–13, 94:7

Isaiah 29:15–16
Galatians 3:10–14; 2 Timothy 2:19

Resistance to sanctification in holiness turns bad.

2 Kings 17:1–18, 17:19–20
Micah 2:6–11
Mark 12:38–40; Luke 12:1–3, 12:13–21, 14:25–33, 22:24–27

50

The great law of love for the Christ breaks forces of hatred.
Beginning in the Church the Lord Jesus wills the holiness of his people,
therefore,
to love the Father and the Spirit also.

Deuteronomy 6:4–5
Psalm 31:23–24
Matthew 22:37; Mark 12:29–30; Luke 10:27a; John 14:21
1 Timothy 6:15–16
1 Peter 1:8–9

The primary obligation of love is:
The commitment of heart to place the Persons of the Trinity first,
whatever the exigencies of life.

\/

The great law of the love of neighbors breaks forces of hate.
The Lord Jesus wills in the Church the holiness of his people,
wherein the love of neighbors also with respect to pollutions.

Exodus 22:21–24, 23:9–11
Leviticus 19:9–11, 19:14, 19:17–18, 19:32, 19:33–34, 23:22
Deuteronomy 15:7–8, 15:11, 24:19–22, 27:18
Matthew 22:39; Mark 12:31a; Luke 10:27b; John 13:34
Romans 13:8–10; Galatians 5:13–15, 6:1–5; Philippians 2:1–11
Hebrews 13:1–6

2 Corinthians 5:17
James 2:8–13
1 Peter 3:8–12, 5:6–11
1 John 2:7–11, 3:11–18, 4:7–12, 5:1

The primary obligation of love is:
the commitment of heart to place neighbors first,
whatever the exigencies of life.

51

The Lord Jesus, through gratitude by way of the Law, builds the redeemed community,
its way of life to meet his holiness.
In holiness he creates renewal in every generation.

Leviticus 18:24–30; Deuteronomy 4:32–40

The Scriptures reveal the way for the generations.

2 Samuel 22:23
Psalms 22:22, 37:5, 77:13
Isaiah 26:7, 30:21, 35:8, 55:6–7
1 Corinthians 12:31
Revelation 21:1–4

The holy way of life glorifies him, the Father, and the Spirit.
Hence,
he presses the Church into sanctification,
and for the interconnectivities of the Kingdom wills that his followers incorporate
—to his glory!—
agricultural, mechanical, and technological inventions.

Joshua 3:5
Proverbs 3:11–12/Hebrews 12:5–6; Proverbs 6:6–11
1 Corinthians 15:58; Ephesians 4:25–32, 5:1–20; 1 Thessalonians 4:9–12; 1 Timothy 5:25, 6:3–10

Hence,
believers work together against assimilation and accommodation;
standing together they refuse any equilibrium:
so much for God, so much for covetous selves.

World conformity has no part in sanctification.
Thus,
beginning in the Church,
and creating the way of life,
on the way into the Eschaton gratitude cuts through sinning.

THE RECREATED ESCHATON

52

At the end of time and history,
with the work that the Trinity set out to do completed,
the Eschaton breaks open.

The Armageddon battle

Jeremiah 1:15–16
Revelation 16:16

The resurrection of the dead

Daniel 12:2
Isaiah 26:19
1 Corinthians 15:50, 15:51–57; 2 Corinthians 4:16—5:10

The final Judgment based on the Golgotha Judgment

Revelation 20:1–3, 20:11–15

The unbelievers' eternal damnation

Psalm 102:25–28
Matthew 25:31–46
Revelation 19:1–6

The marriage feast and the consummation of the Christ and the Bride

1 Corinthians 15:51–57
Revelation 19:6–10

The revelation of the wholeness of the Body,
its 144,000 complete and sanctified

Revelation 7:1–12, 14:1–5

Immortality in holiness

Matthew 25:14–30
Revelation 7:9–12, 14:1–5

See, now, the Bride, the Body, and Flock entering the eternity of holiness.

Revelation 21:1—22:19

\/

In the Eschaton, all in the Spirit's surround see the Christ and the Father
in the glory of holiness.

Matthew 5:8
2 Corinthians 12:1–5

Beloved,
we are God's children now,
and what we will be has not yet appeared,
but we know that when he appears we shall be like him,
because we shall see him as he is.

1 John 3:2

Conclusion

Numbers 6:22–27
Psalm 150:1–6
Romans 11:33–36

*The grace of the Lord Jesus Christ and the love of God
and the fellowship of the Holy Spirit be with you all.*

2 Corinthians 13:14
Ephesians 3:20–21
Jude 24–25
Revelation 22:21

Afterword

In this book, T. Hoogsteen reminds the readers that justification and sanctification are inseparable gifts of redemption because they flow from the unified work of the triune God and his electing, redeeming, and renewing mercy. In justification, our faith results in being forgiven, accepted, and accounted righteous in God's sight. In sanctification, that same faith actively and eagerly takes up all the commands that Christ has given the believers and produces the holiness in the lives of the elect with absolute dependence and obedience to the power of the Holy Spirit which is continually renewing them to reflect Christlikeness, being a living sacrifice, holy and pleasing to God. May THE BRANTFORD CALL evoke the best response in the ecclesia militans to be a constant faithful witness of true faith in the midst of this sinful world today till entering the ecclesia triumphans is my prayer.

Rev. Dr. Yarman Halawa